When I Can't Sleep

KeiAudra Wright

Dedication

Dedicated to my mother and her love and tenderness. Thank you for it all.

<u>Acknowledgment</u>

Thanking my father for his support and believing in me.

A Downward Society

A self-centered world in which we live

Too many bother not to factor in the struggle of the next

Even to those they claim to care so deeply for

Believing, but not knowing for certain, if one understands their trials

Vindictive ways take root and take over to accentuate their lack of empathy

Pretentious antics are no longer tolerated and have grown tiring

Everything in your world is not so deserving of acknowledgment

The hunger for attention and praise are rooted so deeply

They never even take time to ask the other how they are doing

Unfortunately, this cannot be brought to that type of person's attention

Due to an overabundance of excuses and justifications in their arsenal

Rehearsing them in the mirror

With the safety off, they stay ready at all times

Rebuttals on standby to avoid facing the reality of their flaws and that they have them

The result would be catastrophic if that level of consciousness is achieved

A humbling experience

Causing them to lose their false sense of superiority they're convinced they possess

And God forbid such events take place

The direction of the world is one that influences a great sense fear

The magnitude of delicate sensibilities of far too many

The dwindling of absolute guidance

And the extinction of common sense

Not to mention the rapidly increasing rate of the isms of society that has been made a focal point

Were all on a crash course of nothing but the blind leading the blind

Miseducation of words

Their over usage, although mostly out of context

Gives the appearance of trendy and knowledgeable

Topics so many otherwise know nothing about

Failing to realize the word they're using describes them to a tee

And we have social media to thank for it all

Needless to say, it has its perks

But they seem to pale in comparison to the damage that has been inflicted

Producing a realm of followers

The demise of authentic leaders

And children aging but never actually growing

Because the goal is to compete and outdo and not appreciate and grow as a person and care for others

A Troubled Mind

An undeniably underrated, ignored, and belittled condition.

One in which we all suffer.

Whether on a milder scale or the peak of severe

It is a spectrum we wholly hold a standing.

All the money in the world has no bearing.

Neither does career or title.

Ditch the mindset that money solves everything.

If anything, it gives it a stage to show its ass.

No consideration for your class.

That does not matter.

Knowing what to look for

A simple conversation will reveal who suffers from what

And its severity.

Make no mistake these words are more intervention and negative of any judgment.

More educational than critical.

Problems that will not be solved overnight

But if tackled can result in a better quality of life.

Do not let social media trick you into thinking the beauty displayed

Is everything and all you need.

Convincing you that reaching certain levels is a cure.

It is not.

Just because the sun is shining does not mean the weather is warm.

The sun will fool you.

Stay with me.

People with the best careers, greatest success, and seemingly effortless families

Can be some of the most unhappy.

Unintentionally exhibiting these attributes to their children.

Inadvertently distributing them faster than Amazon from A to Z.

Under the impression that kids don't and won't know

When they absolutely do.

They may not have the vocabulary to express what they are seeing

But they know something is not right and will do their best to put it into words.

If not careful, you will see you in them more than you'd like.

Which then makes it easier to figure a solution

But harder to fix because the damage is already done.

Life will take a toll.

The key is to not let it grab a hold and take control.

Let experiences equal out to lessons.

Never forget to recognize your blessings.

Mental illness is as real as it gets.

It is a force to be reckoned with.

A heavy hitter that cannot be ignored.

Keep in mind that pressure busts pipes.

Pills are easier to swallow when they're smaller.

Nothing worth shame.

But is definitely worth the journey.

Go get counseling.

<u>Accent</u>

From kindergarten to twelfth grade everyone's accent is one in the same

We all have a common goal to aspire to

Upon our departure is the beginning of the end

Some fail to lose theirs

They hold firm to it as a child does its favorite toy

Most others' change a multitude of times

As it should

A lot of times it's inevitable

One would prefer the change

Whether they'll acknowledge it or not

Whether they know it or not

Your accent speaks volumes of your growth

It tells where you've been and what you've learned from experiences

It gauges maturity

Just as vocabulary to conversation

Just as glasses to vision

Some accents are meant to be lost

Be mindful of those you surround yourself with

One's accent can be picked up so easily by others

What is referred to as "fake" these days

Is really a matter of two accents that has changed over time

One who no longer thinks as they once did

May come across as a faux version of themself

Especially to those who are basing that individual on the twang they once possessed

A twang they both once spoke in and understood

Do not fault those that succumbed to the evolution

More so pity those who thought not allowing it, in some way, kept them authentic

And losing it would, somehow, decrease their value

When in actuality it has the opposite effect

Increasing one's worth like the housing market during the pandemic in Texas

Avoid fighting the opportunity when it appears

Open your mind to the transformation

The teachings one gathers in the interim

Are building blocks to a destiny you never would have known existed otherwise

A path of uncertainty

Yes

But better than a life of self-induced stagnation

<u>Anhedonia</u>

Having a hard time getting to the depths of life

Unable to comprehend conversations,

Nourish relationships,

Or separate reality from brain fog

Incapable of feeling, let alone, expressing emotions and act accordingly

Feeling like something less than human

Trapped in its own skin

Unbeknownst to me a condition like this never existed

An ailment so complex

Producing numbness to a degree that extends far beyond just mental, but all over

Influencing thoughts at a magnitude greater than any natural disaster

A tasteless hell converting food from necessities to optional

Because satisfaction is nonexistent and so is your appetite

Blunted old memories and being unable to retain new ones

Time blindness causing days to run together

Confusion as to whether one is enduring sunrise or sunset

And the inability to feel pleasure no matter the activity and the profundity of interest

Having emotions is taken for granted

Especially for those consistently angry

Emotions truly make life worth living

Without them, time seems more like a countdown

Filter is now a fictitious malfunctioning mechanism

Resulting in the release of highly undesirable unkindness to whoever wherever over whatever

Usually

So, when I say I don't feel you.

I'm not disagreeing.

Interpreting has morphed from a simple turn of the wheels

Into a strategic process no longer taken place in a matter of seconds

Search the mental rolodex containing a series of past experiences,

Finding one with similarities,

And basing a reaction from that

Operating off of the 'fake it 'til you make it' method for now

More *I, Robot*

And less *Pursuit of Happyness*

To whomever out there suffering

Healing is in the works

<u>Baseline</u>

We hear others' stories and look at some and wonder

How did they get where they are?

People are judged heavily on the nature of their decisions

No one bothers to stop and think what it was based off of or where

It is a mystery to us all where one's mind may end up in the midst of their storm

And it's easy to say what you will and won't do when it's not your back up against the wall

Many have stigmatized the biting of their tongue

In so many cases it has its place

There are two truths

Factual and personal

The latter being opinions

Is spread so recklessly about

The more the mouth is open

The more one's insecurities are displayed

And individuals' flawed way of thinking is amplified

Always bear in mind that one's decisions are birthed from their own experiences

Everyone has a starting point

A baseline in which all are different

Beginnings and Endings

I was 17 years old when I let you go.

Here I am 17 years later.

And I haven't been the same since.

A junior in high school.

One year from official adulthood.

It was a learning experience that sticks with me to this very day.

An occurrence I'm still learning from.

The growth I was forced into 6 years succeeding was one of much difficulty.

In retrospect, some of the thoughts, feelings, and questions still have yet to be answered.

Truthfully, I have changed in ways I'm not proud of.

Often wondering if I could have held onto you longer

Would I be different?

Or would some of the choices I've made been made differently?

Was I supposed to endure the struggles and hardships I've encountered?

Would they have occurred either way?

Who knows!

Once you were gone, life seemed to revolve around you.

There was no crowd I could converse with

Not even a place I could go without you somehow intervening in my contemplations.

Becoming accustomed to not having you, I figured out how to use you to my advantage.

A strategy that worked for us both.

As long as I would stick to the script, I could remain in decent spirits about your absence.

My intuition grew stronger.

I had not a clue what was to become of me or my life.

But so far so good.

I think I'm getting better at it daily.

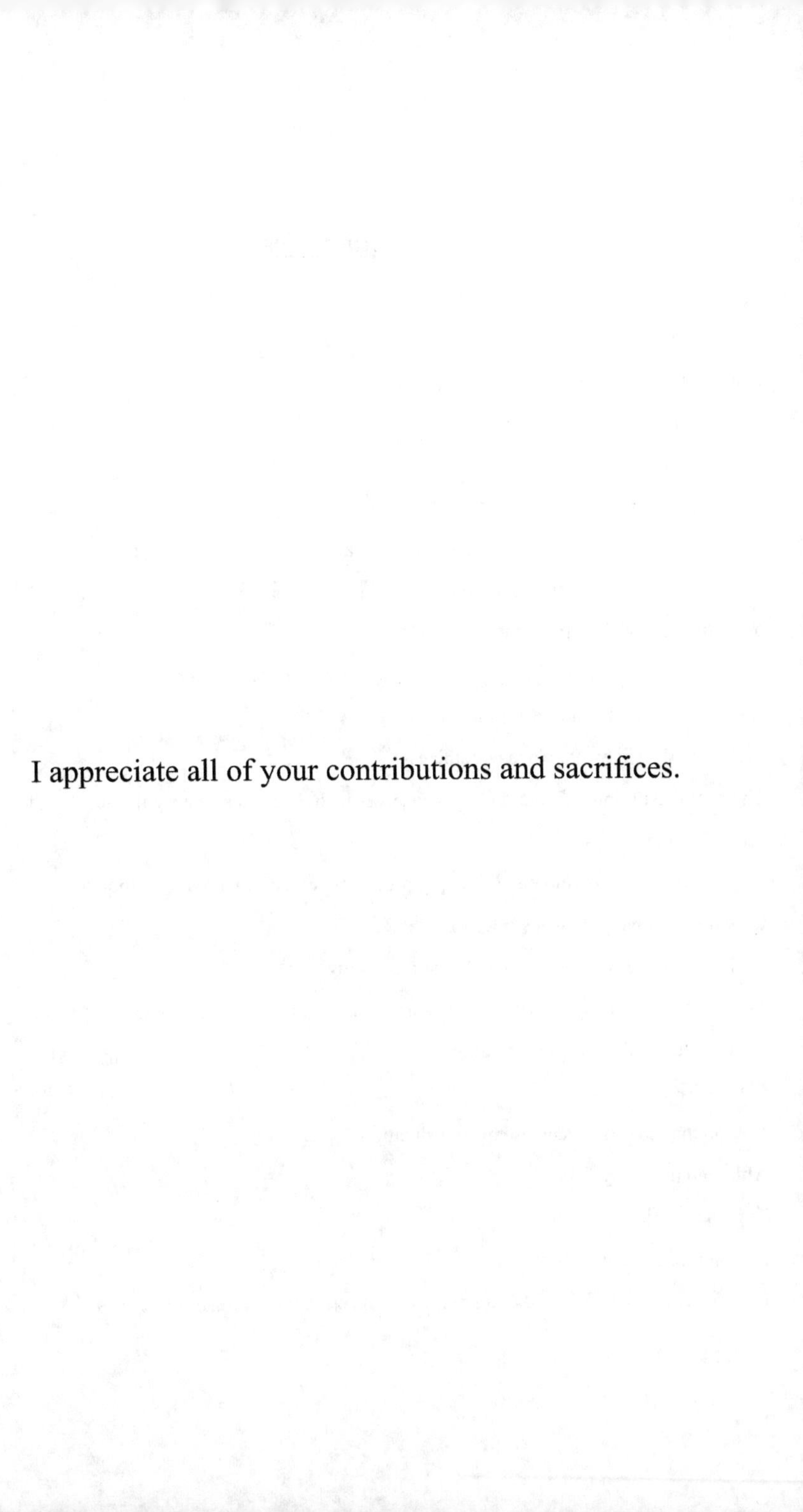

I appreciate all of your contributions and sacrifices.

<u>Boundaries</u>

Let your no mean no

And your yes mean just that

You will find that some people want to treat you

The way they want

Bigger problem lies when they expect you to inarguably accept it

If someone becomes angry because you won't allow them to treat you the way they would like

They need not be in your presence at any point

Your limitations determine the life you lead

Appeasing another not willing to reciprocate is a recipe for disaster

A ship of any sort is not tit for tat

Mutuality does have its place nonetheless

The healthiest thing one can do for themselves is to make clear their wills and won'ts

Their dos and don'ts

Do not fall victim to empathy so deeply rooted in yourself that you overlook #1

Life, not only people, needs rules of conduct

And to not be relied upon to just do the right thing

There are those that exist whom you cannot point out to them their flaws

Unfortunately, that is a losing battle

Mainly for themselves

You on the other hand can escape the situation

Although pain may follow

Time heals all

Reconciliation is an option

Figure out yourself first and prepare for reconnection with a fresh set of eyes

<u>Caged</u>

So many fear the shackles of incarceration

Yet will stay bound to the imprisonment of a relationship in a mentally compromised state

Furthering their susceptibility to more anguish

Dwindling their psyche to a minimum

Neglecting to be honest that they are not who they once were

Whether due to the idea of companionship

Or the fleeing of monophobia

Failing to realize the extent of the damage they possess

To have allowed it to progress this long

And not knowledgeable of their options to rid themselves of the suffering

Living in a prison not allowing for the freeing of their spirit on the level of their choice

Not giving themselves permission to experience this once in a lifetime chance

Functioning at lower frequencies to oblige another

One who would never consider doing the same

This type of prison pales in comparison to any other

Not a soul awakens okay with captivity

Some return to it because it's all they know

Unaware that a love exists beyond anything fathomable

Only it does not show up when the love one shows thyself is bottommost of all

Trying to figure out why they deserve such treatment

A question they must ask while looking in the mirror

Never taught how to love themselves and someone else all at once

Without offering everything

Including a level of devotion and adoration meant solely for their higher power and them

Implementing behavior in desperate need of being unlearned

Showing your true feelings is not wrong

But neither is showing your true self

Under the illusion that as long as they withstand the tortures of this misery

Something of merit will be birthed

Actuality is it will only equate to more torment and a deeper depression

And the sacrificing of the borrowed time allotted to us all

Discontinue this downward spiral of never-ending destruction

Your juice is worth the squeeze and don't forget that

Only you can alter your present and determine what's to come

Everyday bestowed upon you is a reason to celebrate

Do not shorten your gifts for a burden

The only chains that should exist are the ones you have broken

Circumstances

So many have strayed away from just simply being human

No one has the slightest idea of another's day to day struggles

Many have not experienced a situation

Yet issue unsolicited advice that proves to be useless

Mainly because so many other factors come into play when offering "insight"

And I use that term loosely

One may not agree with another's decision

That does not make it right, wrong, or ignorant

It means one is choosing to do what they deem as necessary for their current set of circumstances

Who is anyone to tell them their decision is one of poor taste?

Sometimes one's heart renders them without choices

Their innate nature feels as if any other option will not set well within their spirit

Paths vary and the person experiencing a trying season hardly understands it

What makes someone else think that they will?

Instead of judging one for their choices

Why not, instead, ask how they are doing?

Is there anything I can do to help?

And if you find difficulty in doing either of the gestures listed above

Allow them to vent without criticizing their adversity and how they choose to handle it

Keep in mind that you have no idea what the future holds for you

You may find yourself facing something similar

The universe has its own way of revealing to you how your own ways were not at all beneficial to another

But, in fact, more harmful than not

Strength comes in all shapes and sizes

The very state you believe you will excel in

Can be easily proven that you wouldn't

Simply because it was not a test that was granted to you to overcome

Decently Human

People are going to be who they are.

Accept them for just that.

Attempting to change them into your ideas will only return onto you void.

They will always have too much or too little for the mold you're trying to fit them into.

Perfection is subjective.

Submitting to the status of one's ways will save you in the end.

Allowing you a peace of mind on an immeasurable scale.

A peace so profound that bad days won't seem to be

And good days will be promoted to unsurmountable, pleasure-filled periods.

One will finally know the true definition of cloud nine.

Sweating the small stuff is right up there on the same plateau as accepting others.

So many events take place in life.

Many are frustrating, possible deterrents of your path.

Stay the course.

And when those events find their feats are unsuccessful, they will move on to the next.

Graduating you to be the one educating those who feel this fight is too much.

Serve as a beacon of light for those finding themselves in a dark space.

Inform them that life is not all shimmers and glitz

But bad times are not forever.

Reach back and give to those what you may have lacked.

Guidance.

Positivity.

Support.

Belief that someone is rooting for them to succeed

Just as much as they are rooting for themselves.

Maybe even more.

It is so easy to forget the things that are truly important

And what takes precedence over what.

Try to prioritize your perspectives.

The things that cannot be bought belong in the forefront.

Price tagged items you cannot live without trails right after.

As for everything else if it'll be forgotten on the shelf or closet

Thrown away or handed down as time progresses

Well, you pretty much have your answer.

Do well and all things will follow suit.

Decisions

So few decisions effect only those who decide them.

Easy does it.

The butterfly effect is a real thing.

Be wise about your determinations.

Give them serious thought.

It's one thing to do what's best for you

But burning bridges is not and should never be the goal.

You never know when you might need someone.

At some point you will.

And it will come when you least expect it.

With the tongue being the strongest part of the body

There are times when it's necessary to bite it.

Words cannot be unheard

And contrary to popular belief, they can hurt.

Act unbothered if you want.

We all have a memory of a cringe-worthy comment

That was spewed from the cords of another.

It has stitched itself to our heart like a patch on a quilt

Sewn as a memorial and has helped shape us to be who we are.

As well as vice versa.

Everything has its consequences.

Do not let society post, meme, and reality show you into believing that it is okay or natural.

Spiteful impulses will send you down the trails of regret, misgiving, and doubt.

Although one may tell you they forgive you

It's hard to forget what they're forgiving you for.

Dispose of the mindset of understanding how you influenced someone to feel after the rabbit has the gun

Preventive measures mean making a conscious effort

To filter out your thoughts before they're discharged.

Use your words wisely.

<u>Done</u>

You have the audacity to say I didn't fight to keep you when you made the decision to leave?

Where was the fight to stay?

Knocking down the walls of my heart with battering rams

Such vicious force to enter with ill-intentions.

Because none of them had me or my heart's best interest.

As you remained selfish.

I dug deeper into my selflessness.

Just to discover who I thought was my lover turned out to be none other than a fraud.

Out to make themself and their life more comfortable.

Benefitting from the best parts of me.

Parts that I could've saved for my soulmate which I thought I had done.

Fight to keep you?

Fight to keep the self-absorbed, narcissistic, large amounts of emotional toxicity

Disturbing my peace?

No thank you.

Because let's be honest very few decisions can be made without affecting another.

And as mad as I want to be at you.

The truth is, I allowed it.

So, hell no I'm not fighting.

Be about your way.

The only fighting I'll be doing is to reclaim the me I lost in the process of finding you.

I'll be battling my way back to the tranquility and stillness that seeped out through the cracks of my heart as you charged in like the opposite of a knight and shining armor.

Do not bother to call or send gifts, I am through.

And you're damn right I'll never find another like you.

God would never be so cruel.

Fortifying

To the one praying for my arrival.

I am preparing myself.

Preparing myself to be all that you need.

And most of what you want.

Getting ready to accept your acceptable flaws

With a mentality that's equipped with forgiveness and self-awareness.

Strengthening my ability to express myself to you about any issue.

Minus attitude and passive aggressiveness.

My ultimate goal is to trust in you with all of my essence.

Allow you to lead when presented with the opportunity to do so.

And believe you when you tell me where you were and with whom

Because you have given me no reason not to.

In the meantime, forgive the wait endured by your desire for companionship.

The strides to you necessitates the groundwork listed above.

Due to someone seeing fit that I deserved to be pulled apart.

And I allowed it.

My reassembly is imperative as to not present myself to you

And run the risk of tainting your image of me.

Thus, resulting in an unnecessary and agonizing demise of our relationship.

More so your meter of hope diminishing

Thinking that good women do not exist

And your prayers seemingly returning onto you void.

While you wait, I need you to do the same.

I need your maturity to be honest,

And your integrity to assume the position

Forcing you to remedy the symptoms of failed connections from your past.

Recollecting the faults you and your role possessed.

Be sure to be clear with yourself as to why you are doing this

Along with the ramifications if you choose not to.

Our union and eternity are much anticipated.

Until then…

<u>Getting Back</u>

Taking stock of my life

Facing my challenges like merchandise on shelves

I am strategic in prioritizing the placement of each struggle

The opinions of me are not my burden to bear

Therefore, I will no longer order the product

Who I am is just that

That pill in itself can be hard to swallow

Take with food as to not further upset your delicate already existent imbalance

Social media has distracted so many from their problems

Along the way creating more

Scrolling about just to watch other people live

Why aren't you?

Trying to make heads or tails of the friends from the foes

Becoming easier to differentiate the two

Knowing the truth doesn't make it much easier to part ways

History will have you believing that it's a covenant for life

Outgrowing people is the essence of forward movement

Experiences are supplements for mindsets

We all are deficient in something

Realization, awareness, and the willingness to listen helps with balance

Life is not a one size fits all

Every soul has its flaws and downfalls

Those that say they don't have just displayed theirs

Shifts take place at different times

Clock in and embrace the changes it brings about

Tweak the ones that require it

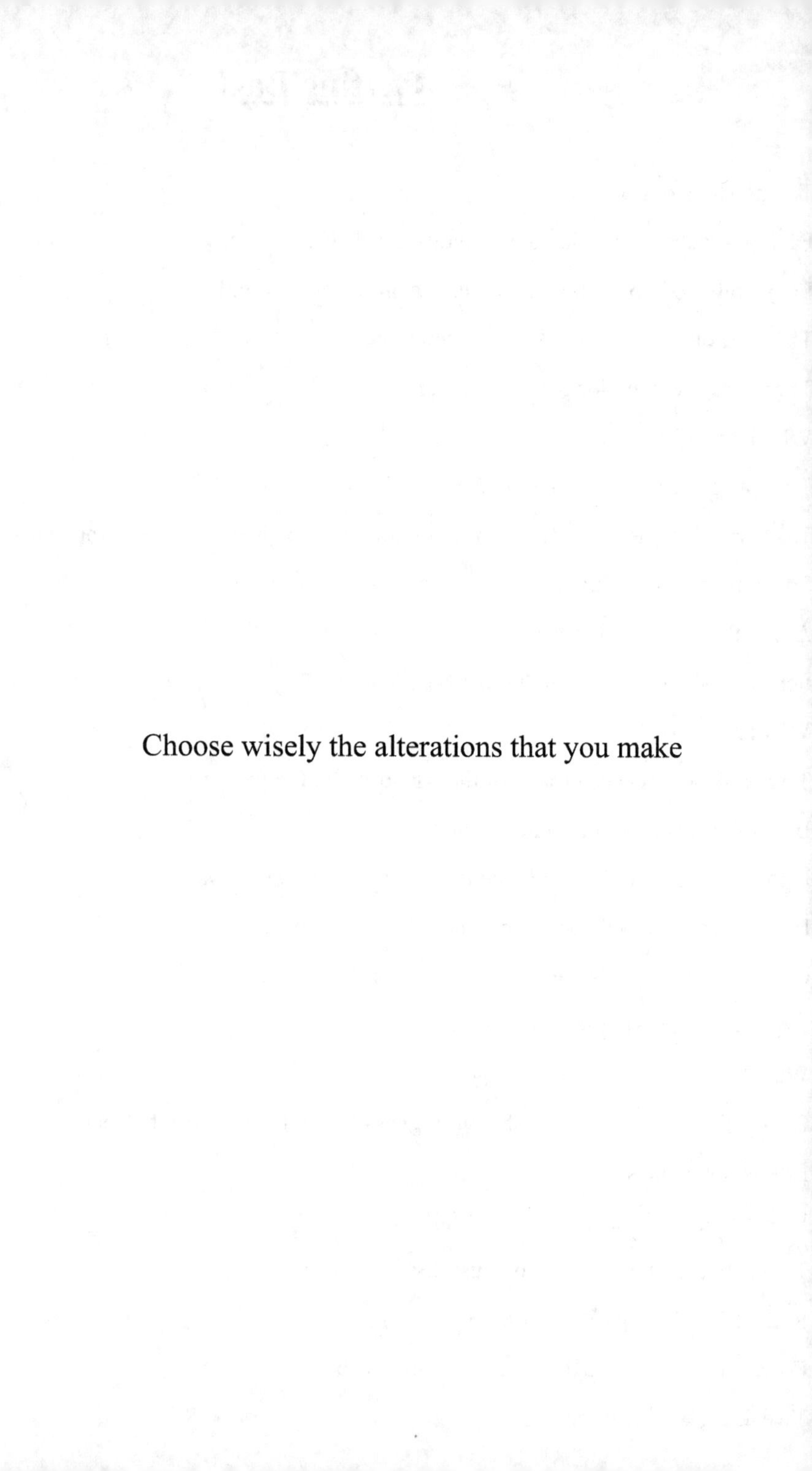

Choose wisely the alterations that you make

Grudges

Darkness lurking in the soul

A build- up of toxins bringing out the worst in a person

Preparing its exit onto anyone you think is showing you similar signals of negative past experiences

But the truth is misery loves company

Letting go of the wrongdoings brought upon you would do more good

Not an easy task to accomplish

I know

Clinging to them is only stunting your character's growth

Embracing negative vibrations that you think are keeping you warm at night

Truly they're only restricting the blood flow to your chakras

Optimism life has to offer you is being blocked

For no good reason other than to assist in building the wall that barricades your access to your future

Harboring resentment like an addict holds tight to their demons

Attempting to justify their habit to continue their binge

The substance makes you feel good, but you know it's not good for you

You've predetermined what's ahead of you when you decide to clutch onto the bitterness that you've fallen victim to and blaming it for your circumstances

Reality is once it's given to you

It is now yours to opt whether to pass or dribble

Accountability is key to forgiveness of others

And yourself

Holding a giveaway sweepstakes, and your power is the prize

Raffling off priceless assets that you have become depleted of

Due to negligence and inconsideration others have influenced you to feel

Contrary to what you may believe you are stronger than that

Life is a gym and struggles are your weights

And the only way to build strength is working them out

Lift baby, lift

Heartache

A pain like no other.

One that rises above the rest.

Reliving the moment produces a tightness in my chest.

An event for the books.

Untouchable if you will.

An experience that confirms that one is not nearly made of steel.

Or am I?!

What does not kill you, makes you stronger.

Is a phrase I've grown to respect and accept

Because a newfound strength I had to reconquer.

People ask does it get easier.

I believe easier is the wrong term.

You grow accustomed to the reality

And there's this living you're forced to relearn.

They'd want you to miss them.

But also continue to live life.

And not carry around this weight that's impossible to lift even with all your might.

Some of the most damaging words I'm sure most dread.

Once they're spoken it makes it damn near impossible to move ahead.

Like learning how to walk all over again.

Except this time you have no desire.

Paralyzing fear of what the first step holds.

You question your ability to maintain control.

One foot in front of the other.

A step at a time.

After time you'll come to discover

The strength that you mustered

Was fueled from the memories she left behind.

It's a wretched moment indeed.

Have yet to find a pill that's harder to swallow.

Years may pass before you're freed.

And it's fine if for a while you feel hollow.

For all who has lost their mother.

Try not to grieve undercover.

Find a friend you can confide.

Please don't try to hide.

You're only asking to continue to suffer.

Healing does take time

But it will happen.

A Human's Obligation

Care for the elderly

They've been through so much

More than we can imagine

We've discovered in our own growth

With age, doesn't always come wisdom

Yet there is still something to be learned

Unbeknownst to you

As aging progresses and child rearing ensues

A lot of us have adapted a state of mind that we know all there is to life

That couldn't be any further from the truth

The wisest man knows that he really knows nothing at all

This is as true today as it was when those words were first spoken

If not for our elders we'd have very little insight on what still needs to be changed and why

When we were told as children that we were the future

Most did not understand the mission

My interpretation is that it is our duty to leave this earth better than we found it

Not just for ourselves

So many have lost sight of that

We're so egotistical and filled with pride that most will not admit this

Too many believe our ways belong to us

The energy of us all make up our daily living

Advancement of technology, the access to knowledge, and the increase in progressive thinking

Allows us to put into play advantages the generation before us was unable to provide for their own superiors

We are to help each other

Including the sick and the ranking

If you feel no obligation in this process that speaks volumes about your moral compass

You know not what the future holds for yourself

And I hope you have a change of heart before that time comes

Humility

The lack of humility is growing by the minute

Some refuse to ask for help as a result

While some others refuse to help because of its absence

Not an issue is it to realize your worth, value, and deservings

The issue lies in immodesty

Paying dues and showing pride in accomplishments and elevations is, in itself, human nature

Excessiveness is the line in which not to cross

Obtainable objects can be stripped just as quickly as acquired

Be cautious with words as they have the power to backfire

Actions do speak louder so make sure the message is one you wouldn't mind being told

I'm Trying

Someone tell me what to do.

With my head to the sky and my knees on the ground.

Arms open, I surrender.

Diagnosed with depression.

Emotionless as ever.

And I don't know where to go from here.

Trudging through the dirt, mud, and trenches.

Lost in the abyss.

Finding difficulty in making the right decision.

But that's exactly what depression is.

Trapped in a downward spiral.

Hitting wall after wall.

No matter how much I keep telling myself to move forward; stand tall.

But it's hard not to crawl.

Everything in adulthood is easier said than done.

Everyone says rid your life of negative energy.

But where do you start?

Where does my energy to complete that task come from?

I'm lost.

Feeling helpless and hopeless.

No one can help me now.

Too far gone without a hand to grasp.

I'm supposed to fix this on my own but how?

So many have advice but no time to assist.

Have I been passed up or all together missed?

Feeling calloused over like fingers plucking the strings of guitars.

Hardened and rigid.

Hoping soon those traits will be indicative,

Of a being pulled from the flames and extinguished.

Generating a tougher exterior and an approach toward life beyond just existing.

Always doing right because it's right, not for good karma or reward.

Burned bridges and bad blood is something I cannot afford.

Giving up is not an option.

Resting is okay.

And knowing the difference is significant.

But even that knowledge doesn't hold solid in setting free the dismay.

Praying for the moment I am unrestricted from this affliction.

Determined to be victorious and a rival of this condition.

I will not give up.

I am trying.

<u>It Will Happen</u>

At some point of time or another

Life has become a bit too extra for us all.

Like standing in the rain uncovered and the crowd watching as apart you fall.

No help is offered and not a hand is lent.

And it takes everything in your power to not pursue how deeply you're spent.

Shifting focus to the day your struggles will be over

Is the only thing convincing enough to stay sober.

Because it's said that bad times don't last always.

The luckless would beg to differ because brakes seem to be for cars and dishes.

But if you can reach down deep and find the fight gene coded in your DNA

You'll realize the days of the future can be rerouted to go a different way.

Understand it is you that gets the final say.

Before you know it, you'll be celebrating your own Independence Day.

Independent because it was your path to progress.

Don't worry about other's opinions; they wouldn't have lasted 2 steps.

The road less traveled is usually the one toward success.

And that alone outweighs the risk of not tapping into the strength you possess.

Know that it'll happen.

Keep Going

Sometimes I question, how I've come as far as I have.

Did a lot of leg work, without a lot of outreaching hands.

At least not helpful ones.

Dug down for strength I had no idea was there.

Considering all my conquered struggles I'm surprised I still have hair.

Don't mind asking for help.

But didn't have a soul to ask.

It's something how those situations give you the motivation you've never had

Although at the time I couldn't see the advantages of my challenges.

Complained more than someone upright and mobile should have been.

I'm grateful for the outcome and how pivotal of a moment those were.

It really comes back down to the corny line we've all heard.

If you give up, you're only giving up on yourself.

Amazingly it's not so cliché once you witness the reviving of your dreams back to health.

Living with yourself after giving up is the part that's hard.

Because dealing with the regrets is a reminder that you didn't play all of your cards.

Having regrets are inevitable.

No one will escape without any.

Just don't allow the regrets you acquire to be birthed from a fear of only not winning.

And if you're vocabulary consists of "what if it doesn't happen"

Keep in mind you have to consider what if it does and keep working towards realizing what you imagine.

Lips

An opening of great magnitude

It can speak life and demise

A main attraction to one's features according to some

Helping to create some of the greatest people to have ever lived

Powers that can be used for good or evil

Many don't know how to channel the energy that lives within

Recklessly spewing material that they deem as facts

When in fact it reeks of uneducated, insensitive opinions

Neglecting to use the final filter to ensure a comment's necessity

Disregarding a person for who they are

Because once it's said it cannot be unsaid

Or unheard for that matter

Apologies lose their value based on their delivery and the deliverer

Sticks and stones may break my bones, but words will never hurt me

Bullshit

Words prey on the psyche

Consuming thoughts and allowing them to run rampant

Concluding deep seated trauma that breeds insecurities

Causing one to question their character and worthiness

Further complicating the existence of those already dealing with mental illness

Which would be everyone

That's why the phrase "mind games" exist

Some perfect the art for fun

But also, as a defense mechanism

Those who fall victim, I pity

No one deserves to suffer the consequences of someone else's lack or shortcomings

Most are unaware that forgiveness is a skill therefore they don't know how to utilize it

And those are the one's at the top of my prayers.

<u>Mama's Pearl</u>

Recalling as a teen asking mama if she could teach me how to cook.

After several failed attempts, I'd only come in the kitchen to take a couple seconds look.

It wasn't my thing, I just really liked to eat.

The last time I asked her, I remember she turned and looked at me.

She said, "When you get hungry enough, you'll learn how to cook."

Little did I know I'd apply those same words to life like a reference book.

How it became relevant to a life in search of success.

Was so outside the box as thinking could get.

After so many moments of finding my thoughts in shambles.

One day it hit me that it was time I take a gamble.

A gamble that would change the direction of my path.

And I realized I could truly be what I wanted with just some simple math.

I'd discover a journey I'm willing to pursue that would feed my passionate hunger.

Then keep hope alive while enjoying the ride on my voyage of wonder.

Within the excursion, I'd strive for a version

Of myself that would be hard to resist.

Once satisfied with this new form and getting a grasp of my new norm

I'll begin to remember what it was like to do more than just exist.

So, if the moral of this story was lost upon you, allow me to set the record straight.

I had grown so tired of the parts of life undesired

And no longer could I permit myself to wait.

In other words, I had gotten so starved, so ravenous, so hungry with the output from life I was getting.

I learned how to cook to nourish my soul and that's how mama's words became so befitting.

Thank you, mama.

<u>Mistreating Yourself</u>

Become okay with saying that today you're not okay.

No need for shame.

Don't be afraid.

Sometimes the skies are gray.

You can fight it all you want.

But healing comes to an open heart.

Autopilot has us lying when anyone asks how you are.

Accustomed to carrying such heavy loads.

Taking on more daily as life unfolds.

Doesn't make it normal because you've done it for so long.

It makes it more concerning that you feel it necessary to be this strong alone.

Couldn't be unhealthier no matter your physical state.

You wonder why your balance is off and why your diet just won't take.

Shoulders are carrying inexplicable weight.

And if that doesn't speak volumes, your cycles are consistently late.

Your body knows your stressed before your mind conceives the notion.

But if you're honest with yourself your thoughts are a cluster of commotion.

If you pay attention, you'll notice that you're a little more impatient.

You're a little more snippy, and little extra lippy and your isolation is becoming second nature.

We all have our days, we're human, this doesn't refer to those.

It's referring to the moments nothing can pull you out of your woes.

So, if nothing else take this, a word to the wise.

I commend your strength, but life is intense, and the one thing you can't do to your subconscious is tell it lies.

<u>Nothing Left to Give</u>

Our companionship was one of sincerity

Or so it was thought to be

Gave so much of myself

Probably more than I should

Bared rose pedaled mornings

Lavender scented peace

Nourished your soul with five-star status sustenance

Tried to be the cool air to your hot day

The warmth to your chills

Words of wisdom that were offered and never requested

Victoria Secret grade support

A small frame with an unstinting heart that would've done her best to catch you if you fall

Levels of love not often seen in this day in age

Showed how to love me by leading by example

Sampling from the mistakes of the past

Innate nature taking over the rest

People speak of love languages as if one has no need to experience them all

Made sure what I presented you with was charcuterie board style of variety

Never expected the exact replica of what I gave

Did expect effort

Your idea of entertainment was all that you found amusing

Neglecting my interests completely

Unappreciation of my many efforts

Taking for granted my offerings

Treating my intentions as obligations

All the while my soul is being starved

Withholding positive gestures out of laziness and inconsideration

Promising me what turned out to be fake diamonds and fake pearls

And I allowed it

Devoid of any energy of benefit

Closing the entrances and exits of my heart

Rejecting incoming affection leery of its capabilities

Denying departure of whatever may be lingering

Ultimately realizing there's nothing to linger

I have nothing left to give

<u>Prayer</u>

My eyes creep open in the morning.

Realizing I'm still here

The first thing I do is thank the One above.

Considering so many lost the luxury between last night and the sun's rising.

Why wouldn't one be grateful for the opportunity to do it again?

Grateful not just on my own behave

But the awakening of those I love.

We all are guilty of partaking in the act of complaining.

Finding difficulty in holding our composure.

The flesh is weak and falling short is inevitable.

Humility is rare and it just takes one to exemplify that behavior.

Headed to my destination and I find myself thankful once again.

Having the comfort of utilizing all my senses rendering me rather self-sufficient.

An attribute taken for granted only by those who know not what they have.

And never having taken the time to imagine what life would be like without it.

Appreciative for the arrival of my relatives to their intended destinations.

Only requesting for their safe travels, arrivals, and during their stay.

Noticing the misfortunes of passerby's, I say a prayer for them.

Praying they find what it is they're seeking within reason.

Giving them satisfaction, hope, and mental clarity.

Extending a little help when I can.

Random moment when I'm relatively sedentary

I feel compelled to donate another thank you just because all is well.

Arriving back at my abode before turning it in for the night

That's right.

One last thanks for a day full of gifts.

Family and I made it back home safe and sound without any problems or interruptions.

Money that was made.

Laughs that were shared.

Other lives that we touched.

The lives that touched us whether we realized it or not.

All those are extras.

Next time you experience the need to complain

Prior to doing so contemplate all that didn't happen.

Recognize that house was not guaranteed to be there upon your arrival.

Grasp that tomorrow did not promise to greet you in the morning.

Prioritize

Emerging into the light.

Squinted eyes; head bowed.

This time I will do it right.

No more selling myself short

Or ignoring my worth.

Too much time spent in the dark

Putting myself on the back burner.

Goals and the present seem to be miles apart.

Devaluing the time borrowed to me

And allowing what I lack to weigh down my ambition to reach for more.

Aspiring for the top, and seemingly glued to the floor.

I will scrape myself loose and accelerate.

Blossoming into my definition of success.

Like reaching another level of puberty

Sprouting an abundance of determination

That former me will pale in comparison to.

Donning a fresh rind that glows of every positive connotation in existence.

My mother did not knuckle down bringing me into this world

Imparting principles

For mediocrity to be the game plan.

That's a slap I'm not willing to partake in.

Motivating everyone else to dream big.

Am I a hypocrite for falling victim to suspected but not full fledge complacency,

But still not quite giving it all I got?

This will change.

Tomorrow I will awaken with the power of a formula one,

The strength of a lion,

Inquisitiveness of a child,

Aim of a sharpshooter,

And seek the patience of Job.

No longer will I be bind by what I don't have.

Instead, I will use that as the dirt to pack under my feet and make me taller.

It will force me to heights higher than top shelf liquor,

And when I arrive, I will know with confidence and conviction

That no obstacle or affliction in creation will ever again make me doubt myself

Or my abilities.

I do have a say and my silence has not served me well.

So, if I seem different

Understand my spirit has been reprogrammed to put me in the forefront.

You mean so much to me

Just not as much as I do to myself.

<u>Pushed</u>

You're so reckless with me.

My love.

My heart.

My spirit.

No matter my methods.

You have managed to take my balances and bounce the checks of my heart leaving me with more debt than I already accumulated.

The all I have given was never reciprocated to any degree

And now you expect me to sit back and continue this road to nothingness and suffering.

Influencing my feelings in ways reminiscent to training lions in the circus.

Some level of abuse to sway my innate and powerful performance to accommodate your entertainment needs

While ensuring I meet the silent manipulative standards you've set for our affiliation

But I will revert back to my inner strength and intensity

Biting back

Fighting back with vengeance and vigilance you've inadvertently instilled and fed all the while

And now no one will be able to save you

You have tranquilized my soul and I am overdue for my awakening.

Old me has died and the new is not fond of your type.

Change is inevitable and it is time for us to go

Splitting ties like illegal cable

Our separation will refuel my core

Birthing an unmedicated rebuild of my character for the world to see

A version so potent when I look in the mirror

The reflection of an intoxicating concentration of resilience and power

With a vision of hope and a forthcoming as vivid as dreams after magnesium

I will not let your psychological haymakers empower you

Like quitting nicotine and coming back to it

It will only reinforce the addiction

And being the heavy bag for your training is completely out of the question

Never being an option to begin with

But by staying I encouraged the behavior that will one day be my testimony

And the weights I build from when I feel I cannot make it.

<u>Remembering</u>

Rhythmic raindrops in a consistent race to the pavement.

Producing questions but no answers.

The elements are against me, or I'm just out of sync with nature.

Are my chakras so unaligned that my wheels are turning with no destination in site?

It feels so.

Withdrawing from humanity every chance I can.

No desire to converse whatsoever.

I used to be full of wits and very clever.

And now my most common phrase is 'Can I get a box of Camel Crush Menthol Silver?'

I've been drained of who I used to be; who I truly am.

Growth is one thing but damn.

Like a man getting out of a cold pool.

Shrinkage is all I know.

No longer is there a glow.

I just want to be me again.

<u>Social Lies</u>

As undeniably informative as the advancement of technology

Specifically, the internet has proven itself to be

Its downfalls are twice as detrimental to

Embedding impossible expectations

Birthing insurmountable levels of low self-esteem

Increasingly chart-topping hills and valleys of mental illness

And the death of a multitude of relationships born out of sincerity

But maintained by the irresponsible guidance of misguided individuals present on the world wide web

Because that's where too many seek for advisement and counseling

For problems that has existed generations longer than social media

And were overcame by the ability of solid communication, common sense, perseverance, and morals

Basing your reactions and rebuttals off of the mannerisms of characters who may or may not act as they portray

Then wondering why things just don't seem to work out in your life

Why long-lasting relationships seem to now be a rarity

Why divorce rates are skyrocketing and happening exponentially sooner than it took for the marriage

And why marriage almost seems like a forbidden misstep

Leaving behind nothing but the fragments and ruins of obliterated relationships that meant so much to you and whose absence changes your life

But society's smoking mirrors has you thinking that the slightest infraction is reason enough to dispose of it to the landfills

Chalking it up to another lost

When ego was the only thing standing in the way of reviving it from the curable disease in which it suffered

Taking trendy rap lyrics to heart

Bypassing the fact that they are meant for entertainment

Hanging on to the words like the phallus that keeps one blinded and stuck

Perfection does not exist, and I don't recommend aspiring to it

Decency should at least be the goal

Everyone hits different plateaus at various times

Don't hinder the process clinging to ideations of dysfunctional media.

<u>Soul</u>

No two are the same

Painting the picture of the human it inhabits

Communicating through arts, acts, and vital moments

Be true to it

Steering you wrong it will not

Interested in knowing it

When something does not feel right one will be alerted

Going against it will only end in regret and possible disaster

It is forgiving

It is healing

It makes one who they are

Innately it directs the body to the nourishment it craves

Feeding it inadequacies can sicken it

Like a vegetarian consuming flesh for the first time

It is strong yet fragile

Throwing off its balance like tightrope walkers

It can lessen one's value

Awareness is the equivalent to control alt delete

Resetting its settings to rid any malfunction unnecessarily present for the willing

Tread lightly

Most times it will heal you before you can destroy it

Sometimes if one is fortunate enough

They'll find another that compliments their own

One that is genuinely bad is hard to come by

Maybe instead misguided due to decisions made without first consulting with it

Or lessons taught along with those that weren't

Start From the Bottom

In order to achieve maximum results

Your base has to reflect a strength unmatched

You have to build on what's solid

And keep in mind that you got it

No matter how hard the blows impact.

Frustration is the sister of discouragement.

She's going to try her hardest to make you give in.

But you ball up your fist

You fight with your might

Keeping in mind that you quitting is her win.

The walls keep you warm; the roof keeps you dry

Those two things are imperative to have

Without one or the other

You'd come out a bit tougher

But a strong foundation is where it begins.

There are a few awarded the luxury of not having to start from scratch

For the majority that's just not the case.

Most will admit

They had no assist

And had to build their own path along the way.

Foundation is everything.

That Old Tape Recorder

I ran across this old tape recorder

That was used for lectures from my college days.

Well sometimes I would forget to turn it off after class

And I'd catch some conversations throughout the day.

Some of the chats were simple and just random hi's and bye's.

Others were somewhat detailed but nothing worth a hide.

One voice in particular I heard was very familiar and caused a smile.

It reminded me how much I missed this girl and how I used to love her lifestyle.

She was pretty damn smart and witty.

Kinda small but not itty bitty.

Conversation whether small or deep was great.

Sometimes she could come off a bit arrogant but to me she was still okay.

Her love for life was one so many wish they could achieve.

Including me.

Hopes and dreams were huge but also well within her means.

If I could see her now, I'd wrap my arms around her tight.

And tell her how much she inspired me and she's why I continue to fight.

She just wouldn't understand how her unwavering ways were so motivating.

Even made harder tasks look painless and new skills she was always cultivating.

Indescribable strength, impeccably well mannered.

Innate ability to help when needed, a sense of humor beyond standard.

What made her the happiest was doing what made her happy.

Listening to music, working out, taking a walk

Reading a book, learning, and her demeanor was pretty swaggy.

The last time we encountered she seemed a bit off and not quite herself.

How I wish someone would've told her how she encourages others, but all withheld.

We all need a bit of reassurance to keep us moving forward.

And I'm pretty sure she needed that at the time.

That's the least she could've been awarded.

Life has a way of taking the good and trying to beat them down to dust.

That's exactly what happened to me but moving forward I must.

I really do miss that young lady.

She was truly one in a million.

If I can admit she was truly legit and always had wonderful resilience.

Continuing to strive for the excellence she owned.

Longing for a lifestyle similar.

Or I would be happy if I could just reach a portion of the potential she had within her.

The young lady I speak so highly of was me in another life.

And if I knew then what I know now I would of pulled her closer and made it a point to keep brightening her light.

I'm making my way back.

<u>Value You</u>

You're worth the fight.

Even if no one has told you or shown you.

Stop begging for love from someone else.

And figure out why you don't hold yourself to the same measures you're expecting.

Find your hobbies, your pastimes, your loves, your passions.

Allow yourself to breathe without someone there to witness it.

It'll serve as a benchmark if you find that you've lost the battle of companionship

Once the pain subsides.

When you ask yourself 'what will I do without them'

Your reminder will be all the good times you had prior to the knowledge of their being.

Following all these folks on Instagram

Chasing behind love.

But find it fearful to chase your own dreams

Focus

If you painted a self-portrait with words

What would serve as your senses?

Would it be a smile, your visions, peace, and experience?

Or the taste of your tears, shrunken eyes, the smell of regret

And encounters with slighted words that served only ill will on the menu?

I hope not.

There's nothing wrong with the pursuit of love

Problem is when you journey pass yourself as a result

Don't make that a habit.

The world has so much good to offer

Permitting the bad to outweigh blazes the trail to unhappiness and remorse.

Who will protect your joy if not you?

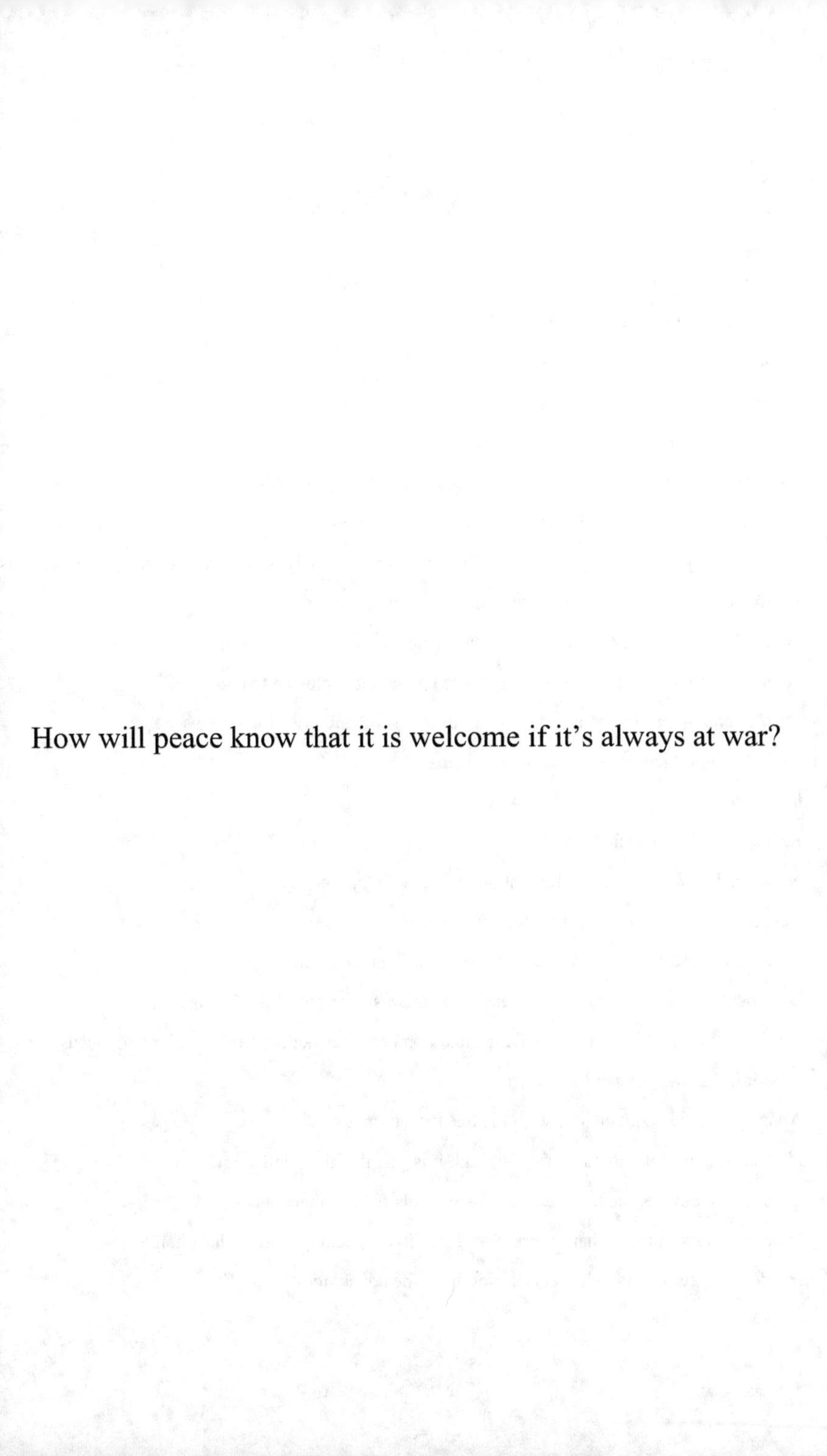
How will peace know that it is welcome if it's always at war?

<u>Wishful Thinking</u>

I weep for the generations to come.

They truly believe they are looking for love

Little are they aware of their lack of bait

Know your worth by all means

But do not tie it to the nonsensical tangibility of life

Nor the pocket-sized, financial acquisitions of another

So many ring out the qualities they seek in a companion

Never do they consider their bringings to the preset table they have laid out in their imagination

Feeling entitled to receive all ticked boxes of their inventory

When they themselves barely scratch the surface of the bare minimum

Neglecting to do any soul searching before becoming exclusive to another

Only to end up on the road to ruins and tainting someone else along the way

Believing that their juice is worth the squeeze

The truth is the fruit went bad long before

Focused on the superficial qualities

Never once did they stop to think about along with that money

Respect and morals need to accompany it

Or with a round derriere also needs to be domesticated abilities

Both parties require a conscience geared toward a strict non- violent pathway

And any other requirements, standards, and compromises necessitating clarity and discussion

Desiring shallow and frivolous attributes

Abandoning the acquaintance with the beauty within

If all criteria is met, what makes you think it is you that they will want?

Growth and development lowers tolerance levels for any inadequacies

No one invests time and hard work into themselves reaching their highest heights

Just to settle for a mate who feels at liberty to the advantages

With no indicators of having also contributed heavy labor into themselves

Too many are seeking outward perfection

And staying blissfully ignorant to the inward damage it comes with

<u>About the Author</u>

KeiAudra's poetry publication *When I Can't Sleep* is even more intriguing than her debut *Inward*. This is a second recognized work that is worth the read.

After receiving her 21st Century Emily Dickinson Award, she knew she had found her rhythm in the poetry world. She displays her point of view on a variety of subjects that speaks volumes to, not only her character and life experiences, but also to the way in which the world would benefit.

Her heart is in her writing, and when she's not writing, she's at the gym, hiking, or spending time with Dukerson Alvin Churchill aka Duke, her 8-year-old, mixed terrier pup.